I0445316

ADVENT
APPELLATIONS

ADVENT APPELLATIONS

The Names Of Jesus That Point To Christmas

KRISTINA HOWARD-BOOTH

Kristina Howard-Booth

Contents

Copyright © 2022 by Kristina Howard-Booth

All rights reserved. No part of this book may be
reproduced in any manner whatsoever without written
permission except in the case of brief quotations
embodied in critical articles and reviews.

First Printing, 2022

Unless otherwise indicated, all Scripture quotations are
from The ESV Bible
(The Holy Bible, English Standard Version), copyright
© 2001 by Crossway,
a publishing ministry of Good News Publishers. Used
by permission. All
rights reserved.

Scripture quotations marked NKJV are taken from The
New King James
Version, copyright © 1982 by Thomas Nelson. Used by
permission. All
rights reserved.

Scripture quotations marked AMPC are taken from
the Amplified Bible
Classic, copyright © 1954, 1958, 1962, 1964, 1965, 1987
by The Lockman
Foundation. Used by permission.

Thank You, Jesus, for being the Good News of great joy for all people.
Merry Christmas!

Introduction

It is my prayer that this Advent devotional will bring you closer to Jesus as you learn about His names and how all of Scripture points to Him. May your Christmas season be filled with the joy that is found in Jesus Christ.

I

Jesus

"you shall call his name Jesus, for
he will save his people from their sins."
Matthew 1:21

Jesus is the reason for the season, so there is no better place to begin Advent than with the name Jesus. The hope and salvation of the world are found in the name of Jesus, "for He will save His people from their sins." In Hebrew, Jesus means "Jehovah the Savior" or "Jehovah is Salvation;" no other name has that kind of power and eternal significance. The angel Gabriel explained this to

Joseph as he told him of Mary's condition, "She will bear a son, and you shall call his name Jesus, for he will save his people from their sins." He also explained to Mary the significance of the name of the son she was to have, "And behold, you will conceive in your womb and bear a son, and you shall call his name Jesus. He will be great and will be called the Son of the Most High. And the Lord God will give to him the throne of his father David, and he will reign over the house of Jacob forever, and of his kingdom there will be no end." (Luke 1:31-33) Salvation was coming; all the promises the Lord had made to His people were going to be fulfilled by the child Mary was going to have, and His name was to announce it all, Jesus. Let us celebrate that Jesus did come; He lived, died, and was resurrected to save us from our sins and to bring us into His eternal kingdom.

PRAYER:

Lord Jesus, we praise Your name. There is no other name that brings hope and salvation to the world. Thank You for being the reason for Christmas, for being our salvation, for loving us enough to come and pay the debt of sin we could never pay. Through Your life, death, and resurrection, You conquered sin, death, and hell for all time, securing eternal salvation for all who follow You. You are on Your throne; You will reign forevermore. Thank You for bringing us into Your kingdom. Thank You for being the name above every other name, Jesus. May we give You all the praise and glory and honor. Amen

2

Wonderful Counselor, Mighty God, Everlasting Father, Prince of Peace

"For to us a child is born, to us a son is given; and the government shall be upon his shoulder, and his name shall be called Wonderful Counselor, Mighty God, Everlasting Father, Prince of Peace."

Isaiah 9:6

In one of the most well-known verses used at Christmas time, you find four of the most compelling, descriptive names of Jesus. The prophet Isaiah described the Messiah and His kingdom that was to come, a kingdom for which the Israelites (and ultimately all people) were longing. It was common during Isaiah's time for kings to have their titles, broadcasting their accomplishments, proclaimed to the people before they would address them. Jesus, the prophesied king, is no different; each title is rooted in His kingship and is being proclaimed before His arrival for all to know Him. We still herald these names, each one depicting a characteristic that could only belong to the Lord Jesus Christ.

Wonderful Counselor references the king's role as the nation's political guide and denotes the personal counsel -- guidance, teaching, comfort – to be given. John Calvin explains, "the Redeemer will come endowed with absolute wisdom...it is not, therefore, because he knows all his father's secrets that the prophet calls him Counselor, but, rather because, preceding from the bosom of the Father, he is in every respect the highest and perfect teacher." (Calvin) Jesus is wisdom incarnate;

He did not run and hide from evil but confronted and conquered it forever on the cross with perfect wisdom. During Advent, we can acknowledge that there is no better counselor, no one who understands life and death better than Jesus. He came to guide us, teach us, and counsel us through every situation we face. "When the cares of my heart are many, your consolations cheer my soul." (Psalm 94:19)

The military strength of Jesus, our Mighty God, is emphasized. Might refers to power in battle; Jesus is undefeated! He has conquered all foes, including sin, hell, and death, because He came in the form of a baby, lived, died, and rose again. Jesus is a warrior and provides us with armor; He is "our strength and shield," protecting us from eternal enemies. (See Ephesians 6) Jesus is our Mighty God, and we do not have to be afraid.

Jesus is eternal. He has always been and always will be; "I am the Alpha and the Omega, the first and the last, the beginning and the end." (Revelation 22:13) Everlasting Father speaks to His eternal nature along with His love and goodness. The passion shown by Jesus as He provides for our needs is more than any earthly parent could give to a child.

Jesus reminds us of this during the Sermon on the Mount; "If you then, who are evil, know how to give good gifts to your children, how much more will your Father who is in heaven give good things to those who ask him!" (Matthew 7:11)

Jesus is the Prince of Peace by virtue of His wonderful counsel, might, and love. Jesus brings peace to His people. "And the angel said to them, 'Fear not, for behold, I bring you good news of great joy that will be for all the people. For unto you is born this day in the city of David a Savior, who is Christ the Lord.'" (Luke 2:10-11) We can attain peace by knowing that our Mighty God, Jesus, has defeated sin and death and is seated on His throne in heaven. Our Everlasting Father has restored our relationship, and one day we will join Him in His eternal kingdom. While we are here, He is our Wonderful Counselor guiding us in all the ways we should go, bringing us hope and peace.

Prayer:

Lord, thousands of years ago, You promised a Wonderful Counselor, Mighty God, Everlasting Father, Prince of Peace, and You fulfilled that promise through Jesus Christ. As we look toward Christmas, we praise You and thank You for Your faithfulness and love. Jesus brings comfort and peace into a chaotic world that desperately needs You. Thank You for Jesus. Amen

3

❦

Son of God

"The beginning of the gospel of Jesus
Christ, the Son of God."
Mark 1:1

Mark wastes no time identifying who Jesus is
and what He has done, emphasizing the impor-
tance of his gospel; it is the good news that changes
everything. This is why we celebrate Christmas.
"The Son of God title was used here to attract at-
tention and secure the respect of those who should
read the gospel. It is no common history. It does
not recount the deals of a man – of a hero or a

philosopher – but the doctrines and doings of the Son of God." (Barnes) For the Jewish people of the time, this title denoted equality with God and was the main characteristic of the Messiah they had been awaiting. Mark quickly backs up his declaration by quoting Malachi and Isaiah and giving a brief account of John the Baptist. John was "the voice of the one crying in the wilderness, "prepare the way of the Lord, make his paths straight" (Mark 1:3) before jumping into the ministry of Jesus.

The foundation of the Gospel, of salvation, of all we believe as Christ-followers is wrapped up in this verse; "The beginning of the gospel of Jesus Christ, the Son of God." Do you recognize that Jesus Christ is the very Son of God? The answer does indeed change everything. Do you need to wrestle with the work Jesus has done? Do you see Christmas for what it is? Jesus, the Son of God, coming into this world, "proclaiming the gospel of God, and saying, 'The time is fulfilled, and the kingdom of God is at hand; repent and believe in the gospel.'" (Mark 1:14-15)

Prayer:

Jesus, here at Christmas time, I thank You, more than ever, for coming to earth, giving up all Your heavenly comfort, yet, staying God while becoming man to save us. You are the One we all search for; You are the Messiah, the Son of God. Amen

4

Elect One

> *"Behold! My Servant whom I uphold,*
> *My Elect One in whom My soul de-*
> *lights! I have put My Spirit upon Him;*
> *He will bring forth justice to the Gen-*
> *tiles."*
>
> *Isaiah 42:1 (NKJV)*

Jesus Christ, the Elect One, was chosen "from all eternity in God's counsels to the great work of man's redemption, and to be the Mediator between God and man." (Exell and Spence-Jones) Do you recognize that Christmas is the day the

Elect One stepped out of eternity to become your Mediator to bring you redemption? As Jesus grew, Isaiah's beautiful prophecy begins to be fulfilled. In particular, at Jesus' baptism, "And when Jesus was baptized, immediately he went up from the water, and behold, the heavens were opened to him, and he saw the Spirit of God descending like a dove and coming to rest on him; and behold, a voice from heaven said, 'This is my beloved Son, with whom I am well pleased.'" (Matthew 3:16-17) Jesus' death and resurrection, which brings salvation to all who believe in Him, Jew and Gentile alike, complete the prophecy. "But now in Christ Jesus, you who once were far off have been brought near by the blood of Christ. For he himself is our peace, who has made us both one and has broken down in his flesh the dividing wall of hostility…So then you are no longer strangers and aliens, but you are fellow citizens with the saints and members of the household of God." (Ephesians 2:13-19)

Prayer:

Lord Jesus, You are the Elect One, The One in whom the Lord delights. You are the One chosen to show all the love of the Lord to the world. We celebrate Your birth, as You stepped out of eternity to join us; so that, Your life, death, and resurrection would bring justice for me, a Gentile, and give me peace and hope. All glory and honor are Yours, Jesus. Thank You. Amen

5

Holy One of Israel

"Fear not, you worm Jacob, you men of Israel! I am the one who helps you, declares the Lord; your Redeemer is the Holy One of Israel."
Isaiah 41:14

The "Holy One of Israel" is the prophet Isaiah's favorite expression for the Lord, using it twenty-five times in just the first five chapters of his book. To be holy is to be set apart, to be completely other; the Lord is so wholly other from us that we can barely begin to understand Him and often despise Him for His holiness. "Ah, sinful nation, a people laden with iniquity, offspring of evildoers, children who deal corruptly! They have forsaken the Lord, they have despised the Holy One of Israel, they are utterly estranged." (Isaiah 1:4) Isaiah's description of the nation and people of Judah sounds as if it could be describing any country in the world today, which can be discouraging. Yet, because "your Redeemer is the Holy One of Israel" there is hope. "Come now, let us reason together, says the Lord: though your sins are like scarlet, they shall be as white as snow; though they are red like crimson, they shall become like wool." (Isaiah 1:18). Jesus Christ washed away the scarlet stains of our sins with the blood He shed on the cross; through His life, death, and resurrection we are cleansed, made "white as snow." Only the Holy One of Israel has that power, only Jesus Christ.

Prayer:

Lord Jesus, You are our Redeemer, the Holy One of Israel. You came into this world to save us. Thank You for loving people who despise You and being willing to come and wash away our sins. You are Holy and Righteous, and it is Your righteous blood that makes me white as snow. Thank You that You are the Holy One of Israel and that we have nothing to fear.

6

Branch

"Hear now, O Joshua the high priest, you and your friends who sit before you, for they are men who are a sign: behold, I will bring my servant the Branch. For behold, on the stone that I have set before Joshua, on a single stone with seven eyes, I will engrave its inscription, declares the Lord of hosts, and I will remove the iniquity of this land in a single day."

Zechariah 3:8-9

Branch is an often-used title by the Old Testament prophets to describe the coming Messiah. Zechariah uses the title as a proper name knowing all those listening would instantly connect the Branch with Isaiah and Jeremiah's descriptive prophecies: "There shall come forth a shoot from the stump of Jesse, and a branch from his roots shall bear fruit." (Isaiah 11:1) "In those days and at that time I will cause a righteous Branch to spring up for David, and he shall execute justice and righteousness in the land." (Jeremiah 33:15) Every reference to the Branch speaks of hope rising from the remnant of the royal line of David, coming from a lowly background to bring righteousness and salvation. In this instance, Zechariah is stating that "from the depressed house of David a scion should spring in whom all that was prophesied concerning the priesthood and kingdom of Israel should find its accomplishment." (Exell and Spence-Jones) The very reason we celebrate Christmas is that Jesus, being born as a baby to parents of a lowly background, did spring up from the remnant of the royal line of David to bring salvation to all people. Jesus, the Branch, became our High Priest fulfilling the high priest's duties once and for all;

"For it was indeed fitting that we should have such a high priest, holy, innocent, unstained, separated from sinners and exalted above the heavens. He has no need, like those high priests, to offer sacrifices daily, first for his own sins and then for those of the people, since he did this once for all when he offered up himself. For the law appoints men in their weakness as high priests, but the word of the oath, which came later than the law, appoints a Son who has been made perfect forever. Now the point in what we are saying is this: we have such a high priest, one who is seated at the right hand of the throne of the Majesty in heaven." (Hebrews 7:26-8:1) As you look at your Christmas tree, consider the branches, as they rise up and point to heaven above. Jesus, through His death on the cross, did indeed "remove the iniquity of this land in a single day;" He is the Branch.

Prayer:

Thank You, Lord Jesus, You are the Branch that arose from the stump of Jesse; You fulfill all the prophecies and promises of the Old Testament. May all the branches of the Christmas trees and wreaths I see, remind me that You brought righteousness and salvation to us, and You will bring justice to us all. The Branch did become the High Priest, and You gave the final sacrifice, Yourself on the cross. The job is completed. You are sitting on Your throne. All glory and honor are Yours.

7

King

> *"Rejoice greatly, O daughter of Zion! Shout aloud, O daughter of Jerusalem! Behold, your king is coming to you; righteous and having salvation is he, humble and mounted on a donkey, on a colt, the foal of a donkey."*
> *Zechariah 9:9*

The King was coming! Advent is our reminder to focus on what it means for Jesus, the King, to come to us. Zechariah's prophecy tells that the King would bring the Jews salvation; He would set them free from all their oppressors and make them a mighty kingdom. Jesus is that King, except His kingdom, is not a temporal, earthly one; His kingdom is eternal. His salvation was not from mere worldly oppression; but from the bondage of sin, death, and hell. Jesus, the King, did come, "They brought the donkey and the colt and put on them their cloaks, and he sat on them. Most of the crowd spread their cloaks on the road, and others cut branches from the trees and spread them on the road. And the crowds that went before him and that followed him were shouting, "Hosanna to the Son of David! Blessed is he who comes in the name of the Lord! Hosanna in the highest!" (Matthew 21:7-9) A week later, that crowd would be shouting and mocking Jesus as He is beaten and crucified, "And over his head, they put the charge against him, which read, "This is Jesus, the King of the Jews." (Matthew 27:37) The people were short-sighted, only thinking of their immediate needs, while the King saw all eternity; "They will make war on the Lamb, and the Lamb will conquer them, for he is Lord of lords and King of kings, and those with him are called and chosen and faithful." (Revelation 17:14)

Prayer:

Jesus, You are the One, True King; we celebrate Your coming at Christmas; may we not forget You the rest of the year. You have conquered every foe and vanquished every enemy, including sin, death, and hell forever. You are King of kings; every knee will bow to You one day. Thank You for being righteous and bringing salvation to me. Hosanna in the highest!

8

Cornerstone

"Therefore thus says the Lord God, 'Behold, I am the one who has laid as a foundation in Zion, a stone, a tested stone, a precious cornerstone, of a sure foundation: 'Whoever believes will not be in haste.'"

Isaiah 28:16

Cornerstones carry the weight of a building; they stabilize and hold together the foundation; Jesus is the Cornerstone of all that the Lord is building. The birth of Jesus ushered in the eternal

Kingdom of God. Jesus carried all the weight of our sins and took the punishment we deserve for them. He is the foundation of salvation and redemption, defeating sin, death, and hell through His life, crucifixion, and resurrection. Jesus is our Cornerstone, our secure foundation, which will not crumble or fade. Peter reminds us of this point in his letter to the exiles: "As you come to him, a living stone rejected by men but in the sight of God chosen and precious, you yourselves like living stones are being built up as a spiritual house, to be a holy priesthood, to offer spiritual sacrifices acceptable to God through Jesus Christ. For it stands in Scripture: "Behold, I am laying in Zion a stone, a cornerstone chosen and precious, and whoever believes in him will not be put to shame." So the honor is for you who believe, but for those who do not believe, "The stone that the builders rejected has become the cornerstone." (1 Peter 2:4-7) Paul also expresses this relationship in his letter to the Ephesians: "So then you are no longer strangers and aliens, but you are fellow citizens with the saints and members of the household of God, built on the foundation of the apostles and prophets, Christ Jesus himself being the cornerstone, in whom the whole structure, being joined together, grows into a holy temple in the Lord." (Ephesians 2:19-21) Building our lives around the Cornerstone, Jesus Christ, means we have nothing to fear. Are you building your life on the Cornerstone of Jesus? Christmas is the perfect time to have a look at your foundation.

Prayer:

Thank You, Jesus, for being my Cornerstone. Nothing life throws at me can cause You to crack or crumble; You carry the weight of salvation as my secure foundation. Eternal life in heaven is definite when founded on You, the chosen and precious Cornerstone. I have nothing to fear, for I will not be put to shame.

9

Mighty One of Jacob

"And you shall know that I, the Lord, am your Savior and your Redeemer, the Mighty One of Jacob."
Isaiah 60:16b

The Mighty One of Jacob is the combining of two titles, Mighty God and God of Jacob. Jacob refers both to the person Jacob, also known as Israel, and the nation of Israel. The God of Jacob is bound by covenant to protect and deliver His people, Israel, for He is the Mighty God and is the only one who can save and redeem them. Advent is our reminder that Jesus is the Mighty One of Jacob; being born as a man, He fulfills the covenants with Abraham, Isaac, and Jacob, redeeming His people from a debt they could never repay and saving them from eternal damnation through His life, death, and resurrection. "And all the prophets who have spoken, from Samuel and those who came after him, also proclaimed these days. You are the sons of the prophets and of the covenant that God made with your fathers, saying to Abraham, 'And in your offspring shall all the families of the earth be blessed.'God, having raised up his servant, sent him to you first, to bless you by turning every one of you from your wickedness." (Acts 3:24-26) Luke records the human genealogy of Jesus, from Joseph back to Adam, in his Gospel account. (see Luke 3:23-38) Jesus is the offspring of Abraham, the Mighty One of Jacob, that turns us from wickedness and gives us the blessings of forgiveness and eternal life.

Prayer:

Mighty One of Jacob, You came; You are our Savior and Redeemer. Jesus, You have delivered

Your people from their sins. You have protected them from eternal damnation. You fulfilled Your covenants. You are the Mighty God, the God of Jacob; You are Lord. Amen

10

Desire and Precious of All Nations

> *"And I will shake all nations and the desire and the precious things of all nations shall come in, and I will fill this house with splendor, says the Lord of hosts."*
>
> *Haggai 2:7 (AMPC)*

"The desire and the precious...of all nations" is a more difficult name to see at first because of how the English language translates the text and adds the word "things" in the middle. The original text had much debate also due to Chamdath "Desire, Precious," a noun in the singular form being paired with bau, "shall come," a plural verb. Is it speaking of material wealth or the Messiah? The answer is both. As with most prophecies, allusions to the material and spiritual reside in the same place. The ancient Jewish interpreters who rendered this phrase stated that the "tile words, in this case, point to a person; and this person can be no one else than the Messiah for whom all nations consciously or unconsciously yearn, in whom all the longings of the human heart find satisfaction." (Exell and Spence-Jones) Matthew Henry expresses the sentiment this way, "desirable to all nations for in him shall all the earth be blessed with the best of blessings; long expected and desired by all believers... this promise is fulfilled in that spiritual peace which Jesus Christ has by his blood purchased for all believers." (Henry)

Jesus, Precious of All Nations, did come; that is why we celebrate Christmas. He shook all the nations; the world has never been the same. "When the Son of Man comes in his glory, and all the angels with him, then he will sit on his glorious throne. Before him will be gathered all the nations" (Matthew 25:31-31a) His house, His kingdom is filled with His glory.

Prayer:

Thank You, Lord Jesus, for coming, for shaking all the nations. You are the Desire and the Precious of All Nations and my heart's Desire. May all the longings of my heart find satisfaction in You. All nations are before You; let Your kingdom be filled with glory, honor, and praise forever.

Lord of Our Righteousness

"In his days Judah will be saved, and Israel will dwell securely. And this is the name by which he will be called: 'The Lord is our righteousness.'"
Jeremiah 23:6

"The Lord Our Righteousness is a sweet name to a convinced sinner; to one that has felt the guilt of sin in his conscience, seen his need of that righteousness, and the worth of it." – Matthew Henry

Jesus Christ is the Lord of Our Righteousness. He was born of a virgin, lived a sinless life, and

He shed His blood on the cross to atone for our sins; He took the wrath of God that we deserve for those sins and covered us with His perfect righteousness. We are made righteous through faith in His life, death, and resurrection. Jesus exchanges His righteousness for our sin "And because of him you are in Christ Jesus, who became to us wisdom from God, righteousness and sanctification and redemption." (1Corinthians 1:30) "By this name every true believer shall call him, and call upon him. We have nothing to plead but this, Christ has died, yea rather is risen again, and we have taken him for our Lord. This righteousness which he was wrought out to the satisfaction of law and justice, becomes ours; being a free gift given to us, through the Spirit of God, who puts it upon us, clothes us with it, enables us to lay hold upon it, and claim an interest in it." (Henry)

Prayer:

Lord Jesus, You are my Righteousness; only through You am I considered righteous and can dwell securely. Your perfect obedience and complete fulfillment of the Law is the righteous covering through which all grace and mercy are given to me. Your righteousness covers me and allows me to have peace with God. It is the free gift for which I do not have enough words to express my gratitude.

12

Man of Sorrows

"He was despised and rejected by men, a man of sorrows and acquainted with grief; and as one from whom men hide their faces, he was despised, and we esteemed him not."

Isaiah 53:3

Isaiah's prophetic words point to the quintessential element of Jesus' relationship with humankind; He was to suffer on behalf of all humanity. Jesus' entire earthly life was a succession of sorrows and sufferings, from the trials of His existence to the continual flow of people in need of physical healing brought before Him. "That evening, they brought to him many who were oppressed by demons, and he cast out the spirits with a word and healed all who were sick. This was to fulfill what was spoken by the prophet Isaiah: 'He took our illnesses and bore our diseases.'" (Matthew 8:16-17) Jesus' intense love and sympathy made Him feel the pain of others as His own, "When Jesus saw her weeping, and the Jews who had come with her also weeping, he was deeply moved in his spirit and greatly troubled. And he said, "Where have you laid him?" They said to him, "Lord, come and see." Jesus wept. So the Jews said, "See how he loved him!" (John 11:33-36) That same love and sympathy would cause Him to come to us, live a sinless life full of sorrow, and endure the excruciating pain and, ultimately, death on the cross to save us from the wrath due to us for our sins. "But now the righteousness of God has been manifested apart from the law, although the Law and the Prophets bear witness to it—the righteousness of God through faith in Jesus Christ for all who believe. For there is no distinction: for all have sinned and fall short of the glory of God, and are justified by his grace as a gift, through the redemption that is in Christ Jesus, whom God put forward as a propitiation by his blood, to be received by faith. This was to show God's righteousness because, in his divine forbearance, he had passed over former sins. It was to show his righteousness at the present time so that he might be just and the justifier of the one who has faith in Jesus." (Romans 3:21-26)

Prayer:

Lord Jesus, I am so sorry You had to suffer for my sins; I cannot begin to thank You for all You have done for me. It is Your love, sympathy, and empathy that make You, Lord. You can relate to all that I go through, and You love me and care for me despite me being a sinner. You lived as a man of sorrows to prove that love to me.

13

The Lord Who Sanctifies

"You are to speak to the people of Israel and say, 'Above all you shall keep my Sabbaths, for this is a sign between me and you throughout your generations, that you may know that I, the Lord, sanctify you."

Exodus 31:13

Sanctification is the process of becoming holy. Only the Lord is Holy; it is who He is; therefore, He cannot be around anyone or anything unholy. The Law served as a way for the people in Old

Testament times that followed it to be sanctified. Unfortunately, like us, they could never keep the law perfectly, and atonement for sin required a sacrifice. The sacrificial system was a continual process as people continually sin. The blood of animals could never cover all sin completely, so the Lord sent Jesus to be the perfect and final sacrifice for sin. Jehovah M'Kaddesh, the Lord who sanctifies does indeed sanctify us. During Advent, remember that it is only because Jesus came and through Jesus' death on the cross, His innocent, sinless life took on the sins of the world (past, present, and future), shedding His blood to cover them once and for all; we are sanctified.

"And by that will we have been sanctified through the offering of the body of Jesus Christ once for all. And every priest stands daily at his service, offering repeatedly the same sacrifices, which can never take away sins. But when Christ had offered for all time a single sacrifice for sins, he sat down at the right hand of God, waiting from that time until his enemies should be made a footstool for his feet. For by a single offering, he has perfected for all time those who are being sanctified. And the Holy Spirit also bears witness to us; for after saying, "This is the covenant that I will make with them after those days, declares the Lord: I will put my laws on their hearts, and write them on their minds," then he adds, "I will remember their sins and their lawless deeds no more." Where there is forgiveness of these, there is no longer any offering for sin. Therefore, brothers, since we have confidence to enter the holy places by the blood of Jesus, by the new and living way that he opened for us through the curtain, that is, through his flesh, and since we have a great priest over the house of God, let us draw near with a true heart in full assurance of faith, with our hearts sprinkled clean from an evil conscience, and our bodies washed with pure water. Let us hold fast the confession of our hope without wavering, for he who promised is faithful." (Hebrews 10:10-23)

Prayer:

Lord Jesus, thank You for being the One who sanctifies me; I could never do it on my own. You have gone before me and have sprinkled my heart clean; so that I can hold fast to the hope found in You, Jehovah M'Kaddesh. Thank You for this beautiful gift that is the reason for Christmas. Thank You for being the perfect and final sacrifice that brings sanctification to all who believe in You. Amen

14

❦

Healer

"for I am the Lord, your healer."
Exodus 15:26

The Lord declared His character to the Israelites as they were in Egypt, protecting them during the plaques, providing Passover, and setting them free; "for I am the Lord that healeth thee; both in body and soul; in body, by preserving from diseases, and by curing them when afflicted with them; and in soul by pardoning their iniquities. " (Gill) Christmas is the ultimate celebration of healing. The Lord, being immutable, does the same for us;

"Now I want to remind you, although you once fully knew it, that Jesus, who saved a people out of the land of Egypt, afterward destroyed those who did not believe." (Jude 5) Jesus cures us, those who have faith in Him, of our most deadly disease, sin. "He himself bore our sins in his body on the tree, that we might die to sin and live to righteousness. By his wounds you have been healed." (1 Peter 2:24) Jesus is our Healer; only through Him is disease and death conquered and healed. "Bless the Lord, O my soul, and forget not all his benefits, who forgives all your iniquity, who heals all your diseases." (Psalm 103:2-3) Because of Jesus, our Healer, we have hope and can trust that one day, "He will wipe away every tear from their eyes, and death shall be no more, neither shall there be mourning, nor crying, nor pain anymore, for the former things have passed away." (Revelation 21:4)

Prayer:

Healer, Jesus, we sing out, "Bless the Lord, O my soul," You have forgiven my iniquity and healed my deadliest disease, "Bless the Lord!" All my hope is found in You; in the future, You have promised, in steadfast love and faithfulness, my Healer, there will be no more pain or mourning. You will wipe away every tear. You heal me, body and soul.

15

Arm of the Lord

"Who has believed what he has heard from us? And to whom has the arm of the Lord been revealed?"
    Isaiah 53:1

The arm is an intricate part of how most function. It is a symbol of power, strength, and might. In Scripture, the Arm of the Lord represents the unlimited active power of the Lord. All of Isaiah 53 speaks of the Arm of the Lord being perfectly revealed in Jesus, "in its grandest operation, creation and the continual sustaining of the universe are great, but redemption is greater...The divine power that is enshrined in Jesus' weakness is power in its widest sweep, for it is to every one that believeth, and in its loftiest purpose, for it is unto salvation." (MacLaren) Jesus' death on the cross, His weakest moment, demonstrated the omnipotence and sovereignty of the Lord. At that moment, the Arm of the Lord bore the wrath all the sins of humanity deserved, defeating sin, death, and hell as He rose again, providing salvation for all who believe in Him. "Oh sing to the Lord a new song, for he has done marvelous things! His right hand and his holy arm have worked salvation for him." (Psalm 98:1)

When you picture Jesus as a baby in the manger, it can be difficult to remember that those sweet, chubby arms would bear the weight of our sins. Consider how Jesus grew, how physically strong His arms would have been as a carpenter; then see the power and protection He covers us with those arms. He is the Arm of the Lord.

Prayer:

Arm of the Lord, I do sing praises for the marvelous things You have done. You are my salvation.

Thank You that in Your weakest moment on earth, You showed Your power and strength; You have defeated sin and death, giving me eternal life.

16

Shoot

*"There shall come forth a shoot
from the stump of Jesse, and a branch
from his roots shall bear fruit."*
Isaiah 11:1

The image of a tender shoot sprouting from the stump of a fallen tree gives so much hope, the hope of renewal and restoration. Israel needed the hope found in this shoot, as do we all; the people of Israel found themselves dispersed, oppressed, and subjugated by many mighty empires; yet, they could hold on to the hope of "a shoot from the stump of Jesse." The Lord was faithful; they knew He would keep His promise; "And the Spirit of the Lord shall rest upon him, the Spirit of wisdom and understanding, the Spirit of counsel and might, the Spirit of knowledge and the fear of the Lord. And his delight shall be in the fear of the Lord. He shall not judge by what his eyes see, or decide disputes by what his ears hear, but with righteousness, he shall judge the poor, and decide with equity for the meek of the earth; and he shall strike the earth with the rod of his mouth, and with the breath of his lips he shall kill the wicked. Righteousness shall be the belt of his waist, and faithfulness the belt of his loins." (Isaiah 11"2-5) Jesus, whose earthly lineage comes directly from King David, son of Jesse, is the Shoot; His very nature is filled with the Spirit, His judgment righteousness, His character faithfulness; all good fruit comes from Him. Let the tender shoots on your Christmas tree be a reminder that Jesus is the fulfillment of all of the Lord's promises.

Prayer:

Lord Jesus, the Shoot from the stump of Jesse, we find hope in You. You did not remain a tender shoot but are a mighty tree of life. You are the vigorous, everlasting vine that connects us to the Father. You are our righteousness; You are our everything. You are faithful.

17

Sunrise

"because of the tender mercy of our God, whereby the sunrise shall visit us from on high to give light to those who sit in darkness and in the shadow of death, to guide our feet into the way of peace."

Luke 1:78-79

How beautifully does the Sunrise express "the tender mercy of our God upon us"? Jesus is the Rising Sun (NIV), the Dayspring (KJV), which gently brightens the sky of our life before bursting over the horizon in magnificent radiance, instantly dissolving the darkness of sin and death when we accept Jesus as our Savior. As humans, we deal with darkness in many forms; but as Christ-followers, "you who fear my name (the Lord), the sun of righteousness (Jesus) shall rise with healing in its wings." (Malachi 4:2 emphasis mine) Only Jesus can fully heal all the wounds of darkness and death "to guide our feet into the way to peace." Once we have the Sunrise, we cannot be entirely overtaken by darkness again. Jesus promised, "I have come into the world as light, so that believers in me may not remain in darkness." (John 12:46) Let each sunrise of Advent remind you of the tender mercy and healing of the Lord.

Prayer:

Thank You, Lord Jesus, for being the Sunrise, for breaking through the darkness of this world to bring us light, healing, mercy, and peace. As the Sun, You are always there, bringing life, and darkness cannot overtake You. You give us new days and new mercies. May we be reminded of You by every sunrise we see. Amen

18

Glory of The Lord

"And the glory of the Lord shall be revealed, and all flesh shall see it together, for the mouth of the Lord has spoken."
Isaiah 40:5

The Glory of the Lord is the manifestation of His presence and of His unique nature. Throughout the Old Testament, the Glory of the Lord was manifest in various forms of light or as a cloud of fire; the emphasis, however, is not on the form but on the absolute power and person of the Lord. In each instance, the Lord revealed a clearer view of His wisdom, power, holiness, mercy, and grace. Jesus is the Light by which the Lord allows us to come face to face with Him; He is the visible revelation of the invisible Lord Almighty, displaying the grace and truth all people need. "And the Word became flesh and dwelt among us, and we have seen his glory, glory as of the only Son from the Father, full of grace and truth." (John 1:14) The cross and resurrection were the ultimate signs of Jesus' divine glory, "But rejoice insofar as you share Christ's sufferings, that you may also rejoice and be glad when his glory is revealed." (1 Peter 4:13) Let every Christmas light you see be a reminder that Jesus is the Glory of the Lord revealed, and there is coming a day "When the Son of Man comes in his glory, and all the angels with him, then he will sit on his glorious throne" (Matthew 25:31), and we will be there to see Him and worship Him forever.

Prayer:

The Glory of the Lord has been revealed; thank You, Jesus, for allowing us to come face to face with Your power, grace, and mercy. You gave Yourself to show us how much You love us. You are the

Glory of the Lord revealed. May every Christmas light we see, remind us of how much we need You. All glory in heaven and earth is Yours.

19

Horn of Salvation

"and has raised up a horn of salvation for us in the house of his servant David,"
Luke 1:69

In Biblical times the horn symbolized strength and might. Advent is the time the Horn trumpets throughout the world, declaring that the Lord brought about His mighty plan of salvation through Jesus Christ, whose life, death, and resurrection conquered sin and death for all eternity. The Lord fulfilled His promise to David; "And

David spoke to the Lord the words of this song on the day when the Lord delivered him from the hand of all his enemies, and from the hand of Saul. He said, 'The Lord is my rock and my fortress and my deliverer, my God, my rock, in whom I take refuge, my shield, and the horn of my salvation, my stronghold and my refuge, my savior; you save me from violence.'" (2 Samuel 22:1-3) Zechariah, a priest and father of John the Baptist, sang about the Lord fulfilling the promise; Jesus Christ, the Horn of Salvation, was about to be born. We should all rejoice as Zechariah did; the Horn of Salvation has risen.

Prayer:

Lord Jesus, Horn of Salvation, may Your trumpet sound throughout the Christmas season. You conquered sin, death, and hell to bring eternal life to those who accept You. You are my Savior in whom I take refuge. May I rejoice and sing of Your strength and might all my days. Amen

Messenger of the Covenant

"And the Lord whom you seek will suddenly come to his temple; and the messenger of the covenant in whom you delight, behold, he is coming, says the Lord of hosts."
Malachi 3:1

The title Messenger of the Covenant is used only once in Scripture, in this last prophecy spoken through Malachi before four hundred years of silence. The promise of the Messenger of the

Covenant is profound. He will be the One who upholds both the Abrahamic Covenant and the Messianic covenant prophesied by Jeremiah and Isaiah. "For this is the covenant that I will make with the house of Israel after those days, declares the Lord: I will put my law within them, and I will write it on their hearts. And I will be their God, and they shall be my people. And no longer shall each one teach his neighbor and each his brother, saying, 'Know the Lord,' for they shall all know me, from the least of them to the greatest, declares the Lord. For I will forgive their iniquity, and I will remember their sin no more." (Jeremiah 31:33-34) Jesus is the Messenger of the Covenant; His birth broke the silence and delivered the new covenant. "Commissioned from his father to bring man home to God by a covenant of grace, who had revolted from him by the violation of the covenant of innocence. By his mediation, this covenant is procured and established; and though he is the prince of the covenant, as some read the clause here, yet he condescended to be the messenger of it, that we might, upon his word, have the fullest assurance of God's goodwill to man." (Benson) Jesus is the One we seek, He did come, and He established a new covenant of grace on the cross. Have you received the Good News of the Messenger of the Covenant?

Prayer:

Lord Jesus, Messenger of the Covenant, thank You for upholding, revealing, and mediating the covenants established by the Lord. You fulfilled the Old Testament's covenants and set a new covenant of grace through Your life, death, and resurrection. Thank You for the grace and mercy You lavish upon me through those covenants.

Redeemer

*"For I know that my Redeemer lives,
and at the last, he will stand upon the
earth."*
Job 19:25

Job declared he had a Redeemer; he trusted that the Lord, his Redeemer, was coming and would right all that was wrong, bringing salvation despite all he had been through. The word translated as Redeemer in the original Hebrew is Goel. Goel was the name given to the next of kin whose duty was to redeem, ransom, or avenge the family member who had fallen into debt or bondage. Job was confident that the Lord would take this duty upon Himself, being surety for him and avenging his quarrel; by the end of Job's life, the Lord had restored him, and Jesus Christ redeemed him completely.

Jesus is our Redeemer; He has pleaded our case before the Lord. He paid the ransom of our sin-debt by shedding His blood on the cross; we are presented blameless through Him. His death and resurrection set us free from the bondage of sin, death, and hell, guaranteeing our eternal salvation. Do you know that your Redeemer lives? Think about what that means as you go through the Christmas season.

Prayer:

My Redeemer, Jesus, is alive, having conquered sin and death; He redeemed me by paying my debt to sin and giving me eternal life. I could thank You from now until I die, and it would never be sufficient to express the thankfulness and gratitude in my heart to You.

22

Son of the Most High

*"He will be great and will be called the
Son of the Most High. And the Lord God
will give to him the throne of his father
David, and he will reign over the house of
Jacob forever, and of his kingdom, there will
be no end."*

Luke 1:32-33

God Most High is the name by which Mel-
chizedek, king, and priest of Salem, referred to the
Lord as he blessed Abram; "And he blessed him
and said, "Blessed be Abram by God Most High,

Possessor of heaven and earth; and blessed be God Most High, who has delivered your enemies into your hand!" And Abram gave him a tenth of everything." (Genesis 14:19-20) The title speaks of God's "absolute perfection in Himself, and His sovereign dominion over all the creatures." (Benson)

Jesus Christ, Son of the Most High, is the fulfillment of God Most High's promise to the people of Israel; "then a throne will be established in steadfast love, and on it will sit in faithfulness in the tent of David one who judges and seeks justice and is swift to do righteousness." (Isaiah 16:5) The Lord, God Most High, was pronouncing Jesus, hundreds of years before He was born, to be His Son and King over all things. Advent is the time when we look toward how the Lord kept His promise and Jesus, Son of the Most High, came and established His throne. This title has always been assigned to Jesus; the demons acknowledge and cower at His power, as demonstrated by the demon that possessed the man at Gerasenes; "And crying out with a loud voice, he said, "What have you to do with me, Jesus, Son of the Most High God? I adjure you by God, do not torment me." (Mark 5:7) Jesus is great, and His kingdom has no end. He is with God and is God (John 1:1). He is the Son of the Most High.

Prayer:

Jesus, You are the Son of the Most High; even the demons know it. Thank You for being the fulfillment of God's promises and for bringing salvation to all who believe in You. Thank You for being the one who "seeks justice and is swift to do righteousness." Thank You that Your kingdom is forever and is "established in steadfast love." Amen

23

Immanuel

"All this took place to fulfill what the Lord had spoken by the prophet: 'Behold, the virgin shall conceive and bear a son, and they shall call his name Immanuel' (which means, God with us)."
Matthew 1:22-23

The name Immanuel or Emmanuel, depending on which Bible translation you are using, is a combination of two words; "El," God, and "emmanu," with us; to unmistakably mean "God with us." In the Hebrew Bible, Yahweh, the Lord, tells

His people, "I am with you" one hundred fourteen times. With the arrival of Jesus, which can be translated as Yahweh saves, the Lord declares, after four hundred years of silence, "I am with you. My divine presence is physically among you." Reminding the people that He had never left them, He faithfully fulfilled the promise He made to king Ahaz through the prophet Isaiah seven hundred years before. "And he said, "Hear then, O house of David! Is it too little for you to weary men, that you weary my God also? Therefore the Lord himself will give you a sign. Behold, the virgin shall conceive and bear a son, and shall call his name Immanuel." (Isaiah 7:13-14)

Christmas is the celebration that God is still with us, even though we may feel that we are experiencing long periods of silence like the Israelites. Remember, the Lord never left them. He was at work getting everything ready for His perfect timing to reveal the best opportunity for their life to have maximum impact. Jesus' birth was at the perfect time to change the world. Immanuel, God is with us.

Prayer:

Lord, Immanuel, it is an overwhelming comfort to know that you are with us, always. When we feel alone, we can trust that You are there. When we think all is silence, we can trust that You are still by our side, working things out for our good. Thank You for always being with us. Amen

24

Savior

"And the angel said to them, "Fear not, for behold, I bring you good news of great joy that will be for all the people. For unto you is born this day in the city of David a Savior,"
Luke 2:10-11a

Christmas is all about salvation. The Lord loves us so much that He sent a Savior to deliver us from the wrath and death we deserve. Savior is a distinctive title, instantly generating images of God saving and delivering His people. The Gospel, according to Luke, focuses on the grace, mercy, power, and authority of Jesus as Savior. Mary and Zechariah acknowledge their need for a savior before Jesus' birth and praised the Lord for what He was going to do through Him: "Blessed be the Lord God of Israel, for he has visited and redeemed his people and has raised up a horn of salvation for us in the house of his servant David… And you, child, will be called the prophet of the Most High; for you will go before the Lord to prepare his ways, to give knowledge of salvation to his people in the forgiveness of their sins, because of the tender mercy of our God." (Luke 1:68-78a) Simeon and Anna acknowledge Jesus as Savior when He is brought to the temple as a baby exclaiming, "Lord, now you are letting your servant depart in peace, according to your word; for my eyes have seen your salvation that you have prepared in the presence of all peoples… And coming up at that very hour, she began to give thanks to God and to speak of him to all who were waiting for the redemption of Jerusalem." (Luke 2:29-38) The Savior they had been waiting for had arrived. He is our Savior also, "his name is called Jesus, because He saves from sin, from Satan, from the law, from the world, from death, and hell, and wrath to come and from every enemy." (Gill) Celebrate the Good News; "And Jesus said to him, "Today salvation has come to this house, since he also is a son of Abraham. For the Son of Man came to seek and to save the lost." (Luke 19:9-10)

Prayer:

Savior, we worship You and praise You for all You have done for us. Christmas should remind us that You were born to be our Savior. You have saved us from sin, death, and hell. You have covered us in Your righteousness. Jesus, You love us enough to come and save us. Thank You for Your mercy, grace, and love. Amen

25

Christ

*"For unto you is born this day
in the city of David a Savior, who
is Christ the Lord."*
Luke 2:11

There is no Christmas without Christ. The
hope and power wrapped up in the title "Christ"
is immense; it is the "good news of great joy that
will be for all the people." (Luke 2:10) The Christ,
the Messiah, was about to be born. Christos, the
Greek word from which we get Christ, is the
Greek translation of the Hebrew word Messiah; it

occurs over five hundred times in the Greek New Testament as the designated title for Jesus. Christ the Lord implies, "the Messiah spoken of by the prophets; the anointed of the Lord, with the Holy Ghost without measure, to be a prophet, priest, and king in his church; and who is the true Jehovah, the Lord our righteousness, the Lord of all creatures, the Lord of angels, good and bad, the Lord of all men, as Creator, the Prince of the kings of the earth, the Lord of lords, and King of kings." (Gill) Jesus is Christ; He is the promised Messiah fulfilled. Celebrate the Good News!

Prayer:

Christ Jesus, You are "the good news of great joy," You are the Messiah, the deliverer of all people, our salvation. Great is Your name and worthy of all our praise. May You receive all glory and honor as Christ the Lord! Amen

References

Barnes, Albert. "Barnes' Notes on the Whole Bible." 1870. *Bible Hub.* 22 November 2020.

Benson, Joseph. "Commentary on Malachi 3." 1857. *studylight.org.* 18 July 2021.

Calvin, John. "Calvin's Commentaries." n.d. *Bible Hub.* 15 October 2020.

Exell, Joseph S and Henry Donald Maurice. Spence-Jones. "Commentary on Isaiah 42. The Pulpit Commentary." 1897. *StudyLight.org.* 28 11 2021.

Gill, John. "Commentary on Exodus 15." 1999. *The New John Gill Exposition of the Entire Bible.* 28 October 2020.

Henry, Matthew. 1706. *Matthew Henry's Complete Commentary on the Whole Bible.* November 8 2021.

MacLaren, Alexander. "Alexander MacLaren's Expositions of Holy Scripture." n.d. *studylight.org.* 3 September 2021.

www.ingramcontent.com/pod-product-compliance
Lightning Source LLC
Chambersburg PA
CBHW060347130626
46553CB00003B/1114